THE FIRST EARTHQUAKE

BY THE SAME AUTHOR

POETRY

The Collector and Other Poems
The Nature of Cold Weather and Other Poems
At the White Monument and Other Poems
The Force and Other Poems
Work in Progress
Dr Faust's Sea-Spirit and Other Poems
Three Pieces for Voices
The Hermaphrodite Album (with Penelope Shuttle)
Sons of My Skin: Selected Poems 1954–74
From Every Chink of the Ark
The Weddings at Nether Powers
The Apple-Broadcast and Other New Poems
The Working of Water
The Man Named East and Other New Poems
The Mudlark Poems & Grand Buveur
The Moon Disposes: Poems 1954–1987
In the Hall of the Saurians

FICTION

In the Country of the Skin
The Terrors of Dr Treviles (with Penelope Shuttle)
The Glass Cottage
The God of Glass
The Sleep of the Great Hypnotist
The Beekeepers
The Facilitators, or, Madam Hole-in-the-Day
The One Who Set Out to Study Fear

PLAYBOOKS

Miss Carstairs Dressed for Blooding and Other Plays
In the Country of the Skin

PSYCHOLOGY AND SOCIOLOGY

The Wise Wound (with Penelope Shuttle)
The Black Goddess and the Sixth Sense

THE FIRST EARTHQUAKE

PETER REDGROVE

Secker & Warburg
POETRY

First published in Great Britain 1989 by
Martin Secker & Warburg Limited
Michelin House, 81 Fulham Road,
London SW3 6RB

A CIP catalogue record for this book
is available from the British Library

ISBN 0 436 41006 0

Printed and bound in Great Britain by
Redwood Burn Limited, Trowbridge, Wiltshire

CONTENTS

ACKNOWLEDGEMENTS

Acknowledgements are due to the following:

Cornish Banner, *Encounter*, *Manhattan Review*, *Outposts*, *Oxford Poetry*, *P.E.N. New Poetry 1*, *Poetry Australia*, *Poetry Review*, *Poetry Book Society Supplement 1984*, *Prospice*, *The Rialto*, *Slightly Soiled*, *Stand*, *Sunday Times*, *Temenos*, *Times Literary Supplement*, *Westwords*, *Words International*

'The First Earthquake' was first published as a pamphlet by Sceptre Press.

THE FIRST EARTHQUAKE

The birds squabbled and fell silent
In their million trees like colleges of monks
With their mean little ways and their beautiful songs;

The yachts like moored forests,
The yachts rocked in their haven
Like women in long dresses

And invisible feet
Bowing to the earthquake.
The mist had rolled in

And developed all the spiderwebs,
The trees in the groves draped
Like pearl-sewn yachts,

The million spiders in them asleep,
The spiders in their white roofs,
The dew-lapping spiders,

They nodded their toolchest faces,
Beards wet with dew,
Dew brimming their webs and their claws;

Complex water shivered everywhere like a single ghost.
Lovers, smelling of almonds and new bread,
Roused from their beds, pointed

Rubbing their eyes at the copses of yachts
That tugged at the tremor and dipped,
Shivering rain from their tackles,

Lovers who shivered like silk
As the rafters groaned
Within their white ceilings,

This earthquake shoved up fifty new fountains!
After the first shock we are ravenous,
The little silvery fishes grizzling in the shiny pans.

LADY READERS IN PENAL CHILDBIRTH

I

All the women who were hanged
Had one soul
Which now returns;
The tree shaken at dawn,
The ghosts passing like dew.

And some were with child,
And the hanging postponed
So that they could be born
And the mother hanged after.
These were called 'Infants of the State',
The mother in 'penal childbirth'.

What revenge could ever be made for this!
The soul of mother and child
Would be for ever
In penal servitude of revenge.

II

On the tube I see a Chinese man reading a paperback
Pleasures of the Torture-Chamber
As the city speeds past,
The station-pages speeding past.
We alight at a new chapter.

III

Those women sitting on the underground
They wear the rope-bruise round their necks,
Each has a child by a rope
Attached to her still;
A woman leans over, her breath smells of dust,
We should live as though we were reading, she says,
And prize our ability to put the book down
If it grows too vengeful;
When the story catches
You incarnate dangerously;
No one should shut herself
Inside her book.

IV

I open a page of the timetable,
A small fly is flattened into a letter,
A snot-sized letter,
Its juices adsorbed through several pages' stain
In recurrent inscription.
The book as spider-web.

The train is full of lady readers,
They wear chokers
As if to conceal hanging bruises.

Revenge? I ask.
Read on, she replies.

SUMMER

I

The summer mice are fat as butter.
There is the waste of a silent bronze-smithy,
Tightly-curled lathings, and the everlasting

Scent of brass.
There is a fly listening to an egg in the kitchen.
There is a child sipping warm blood in the womb,

In the hot bell-fat womb.
Auntie holds up the smoothing-iron
Polished like a mirror with its work,

She looks into it and spits,
It satisfies, she peels
The knife-edged denim off the ironing board;

It satisfies, his tomorrow's shirt,
Blue as the sky faded with its clouds;
And as the river goes to bed in leaves,

In ten billion leaves flowing through the summer,
So must the nephew sink into the feather-bed upstairs,
Wallow in its lavender laundered marsh.

II

The nephew sunk in the feather-bed upstairs,
Nesting for summer in this feather-bed,
Dreams of the women of the house that all night

They braid their hair and chat
And sweep the kitchen for tomorrow's chores
And they never go to bed at all,

Since they are still there in the morning frying breakfast.
Munching his fried bread with shining lips,
His smile pocked and sintered like cuttlebone,

The uncle rubs his big hands in the boy's hair.

III

Past the river jammed like corduroy with logs
Which have been there so long their shoots
Are bushing into hedgerows, locking them,

There is a bluebell-wood by mudflats
And within it a comb of soft long meadow that delves
Into a flank of Shivering Mountain;

The shuddering cloud-shapes shake over it,
The small springs shiver down its slopes,
The scree slips day and night a little,

Expanding in the hot sun and holding,
Slipping a little further in oily dew of evening.

IV

The shades that pour down Shivering Mountain
Are irresistible to me,
Its grey locks, cloud canopy,

Its cap of invisibility;
I climb into insubstantiality
Like an old Chinese effacing among his chasms

Sliding through empty ghost rock-cities
Repopulated suddenly with shades.
I am not an old Chinese for long;

My uncle comes with dogs and shotguns looking for me,
And slaps me back into his world,
And cuffs me down slippery scree with his grinning acne,

With a pock-mask like the bottom of the sea.

THE CAPSULES

The various capsules, variegated
With their grains
Mingling pink within gelatine tabernacles;

The gross brown capsules
Fizzing with their handles:
The pints;

The long white tabsule of nicotine and fire,
Parks of the lungs browning like autumn,
Like bonfires approaching:

A whitewashed path white as a peeled staff
Along which
A bonfire approaches coughing;

I watch the young man being curried
Into feeling by the tobacconist's assistant
Despite the daily necklaces of medicines;

It is like the ugly beauty of gargoyles
Through which
The blessed rain flows; it is like

The long cool violin-face of the horse, laid
Along the drystone wall
Drinking the dry stones' shadow like water;

It is like the oil-rigs lighted,
Populous cities,
Their seminal oil pumped from retirement in the old depths,

Spill it a little,
And the entire sea washes whole in one round rainbow.

UNDER NELSON'S EYE

Under the stiff column of Nelson he offers his bread
To the doves, 'Lalilai,' they go, 'Lalilai,'
In bass, 'here comes a priest who has repented,
He has brought us a brown paper bag of bread
Of Jesus which he feeds us, lalilai, lalilai;'
Communion with the animals is effected
And will wing its way through the world
But so many come there is not enough holiness in his bag
So they eat him to find it, bloody bundle
Levitated on a thousand wings six feet off the ground
At head-height, they lift him up in a cloud
Raining blood and wheel up Whitehall clearing the Cenotaph.

OF PRICKBUSH

Most archaic plant, or prickbush, the holly,
Bluish-green when immature,
The sheen of corpses as they start to travel
The insect-path, colour
Of duality, the ocean and the sky.

There is much holly on these quarry cliffs,
Blocks of dynamited stone, rusty rails
Like stitched wounds, and the trees which prise
More stone with their slow green dynamitings,
And the west gulf packed with prickbush.
An apple-tree fruits at the whiskery lip,
A shower of fruit falls
Into the holly-bushes where the birds find refuge
In their dark green attics;
Separated by the prickly walls, these birds
Become individuals and sing for themselves, yet chime.

Most archaic plant, the mother holly
Is the first house, her doll of holly wood
The kern baby, signifying the seed
Or kernel of future harvest,
And the heaven at the centre of the tree
Where the birds sing
Like the repeaters of life
And nest in the prickly dark land of song.

AT DELABOLE QUARRY

The slate like pages
Of a precipice-book glinting everywhere
With stars of quartz:
A work of astronomy with the
Whole abyss mapped on it,
The earth sketching
Itself on its own slate.

My wholeness aroused
I was nearly lost
In the slate tabernacle
(The Cleave Horse
In the Stables of Slate)
As if it were the place
Where the Blessed contemplate
Form as leaves of slate
On a still tree;

They watch their nature
Be what it may, for
However struck, slate
Presents a perfect sheer,
The loose tables shining
Like great rhomboid coins
Impossible to pocket;
Under that gaze the spectator shrinks
To a name carved on a slate
For throughout the world
Churchyard lichens scroll their Delabole
With crispy annotations
And out of this chasm come
Roofs for the living and

Slate books of one page for the dead . . .
Shout into this canyon,
It is too big to echo
Yet a whisper
Flies quick as a bird
Desiring to write
The capacity and exactitude
Of slate, the shape
Of its abyss, everywhere.

GLITTERING PHARMACY

Pounding much glittering medicine
I and the pharmacist, pounding,
My young pestle in the mortar of hair;

Perfume and a substance that is
Beyond flesh. With the sleeve
Of my white coat

I had snagged a magistery from its shelf;
It smashed, but into self-remembering vapours
Knitting together and copulating about us,

The sculptured jar recomposed itself
On the shelf, to the nose invulnerable.
It made the dark woman kiss me,

The dark woman in the white coat
With lips red enough to pronounce
Every magical name resounding

And arrayed across each porcelain tub:
A shop of vaporous gingers and catspaw ethers
Playing with us to exhaustion;

It was the magic shop
Of medicine made us kiss,
Equilibrating the forces,

I the science-mad twelve-year-old,
And she the MPS of thirty. 'Why
Did you kiss me?' I enquired, and that made her

Laugh like *Pulv. Zingiber* and *Ol. Aurant*,
Scammony and *Ficus Comp*.

HARVEST

I

The greatest possible touch, to bathe.
The wind bathing in the wheat,
The great invisible woman plunges
Into the heavy tassels, into the wheat-smell
That is like straw baskets full of new bread;
The wheat splashes round her, it must cry out,
All the stems chafing, like an immense piano plunged into
Which continues playing as she swims,
A piano full of wheat, a concert grand
Whose blackness opened on a field of wheat
And the music swims in it, and in wide waves descants;
She does the overarm crawl from one stone hedge
To the far end, and climbs out, invisible, dripping with rain.

II

As though all the wheat in the world
Were her hair, in which she bathes.

III

The Miners' Brass Band concurs,
They are a procession of buttery lotuses,
The sunlit air pours into them
And coils around their instruments
Like lotuses evolving from their lungs
In the sound of mined metal vibrating
With human breath, earth and air
Married: its child, music.
I wonder if the great churches
And concert halls mark standing waves
Where the weather stills as over mines
And you can blow your golden lotus and be heard.

III

The metal walks and sings. Pausing
Halfway up the house stairs
I can hear the two radio sets at once
Tuned to the same music; we call that 'The Well',
A well of music sounding between two floors.
At present we have a well-known soloist
Playing with an anonymous orchestra
Unknown to him.

I think of a buck-naked
Skinny young fellow at the piano
The sunwarmed air of the music
Like a golden wheatfield brothing around him.

TO THE BLACK POET

I

The lightning flashes
Over her silk suit, the silk
In repose in which she dreams;
Now I am afraid she is out in
The garden, out in the rain,
In her pyjamas, again; and her skin
Jealous for that silk especially;

It is a bad sign the evening before
When she dons the stiff broadcloth trousers;
I am bound to find her wet
Out in the garden in white silk
That next morning. It was in silk

Open at the legs
She gripped her birth-pangs
As the Goddess gripped mountains; I stood by
Awaiting her pleasure and passed the time
Considering the tank where the fish glide
Kissing the water as they swim, their lips
Rosed by the tropics.

II

She has invited her lover
The famous black poet
Whose beauty she told me
Was in his nostrils
Which expand marvellously
As he inhales to speak poetry;

There is no filthy rubble
In there, no kind of
Misshapen surprise, no hard
Facial shit in such a nose.

III

One can stare deep into it
Without fear, inhaling
The sweet smell of his discourse;
She swears it was how she conceived.
It is rose-coloured up there
A rose twilight in black depths
Blowing with articulate winds
The raw material of his poetry speech,
A breath like a marvellous
Air of the tropics reversing in a black conch
Scented with hibiscus and mango-sweat.

IV

She says, It is for longing
Of him that I go out in white silk
To stare up into the southern rain
In the rose-coloured dusk
To feel it clasp my body's form
As it slowly falls, in my pyjamas
Like a warm bed-embrace.
It is scented with the perspiration of mangoes;
I inhale that rain
Into my caves of poetry,
Our child will strip me off
Like silk clothes drenched with labour;
It will sneeze me out of its black conched caverns.

V

It is my privilege to know him
To stare into his nose
And listen to his mouth,
To be surrounded by his tropic air,
And, instead of having to meet
Him in the eye, as with the pink men,

To greet him by staring deep
Into his insufflating nose, his place
Of inspiration, myself a whole skin
Silk bandana to his spermatic sneeze.

WATCHING

A boy's long hair
That does not look girlish
To the girls. He knows
How to box the compass,
How to nail the four quarters down.
He pisses like a gentleman among the trees
With his long hair blazing like a flume,
His jet blazes like a flame
The salt sea-wind cannot put out, he does up
His sailor's flap with the six buttons
Like a Constellation named 'The Trousers'.
He is all Constellation, with his shirt and hair.

There pass by him whistling
As he pisses his warm jet among the trees
Three women who sport various dresses
But who wear identical pairs of white shoes;
They step past like one insect,
And like one body they laugh and ripple,

Which is their challenge to the boy,
His long hair clustered like a high collar.
He is sure he knows how to cross that river
Made of the three women and their choppy waves,
The water of the three women. As for myself
From under my bald pate I watch the comedy,
I have bad teeth and tattered clothing,
I am a very suspicious character, stopped
To watch the women,
Who walk past and smile with courtesy
Like the one identical insect, even at me; now I must
Go home and change my clothing
For every garment

Is a clause in the personal sentence
And I cannot be sure they have read there
'Ferryman willing to punt across Broads
In the direst weather.'

UNDERTAKER'S WIND

I

Someone was climbing the pepper-tree;
We let them.
The fig-tree grew out of the cellar;
We let it.

II

The knife used as a book-mark,
The slender knife light,
The book weighty;
In the gutter of the book
Ancient headlines
'Spiritualist Murders Bride';
This tree climbs about our minds.

III

The massive odour of sex
About the whole house,
Building its own sliding casements,
Its doors swinging in the breeze.

The unrefreshing East Wind
Stunting the trees;
It is like a breeze in reverse,
It is a suction
Like the kiss of a man
A spiritualist maybe
Starved for bodies,
Yearning for his bride.

It is a wind with mouths in it.

IV

It is the ambience of the East Wind
Which knocks the wasps down,
One had mistaken her beer
For its paper nest in the amber city which hums,
Going for the gleam in the beer
Went for its rest in her alcohol,
The angry wasp;
She bent over it amused and appalled
'How shall we rescue it?'
Fishing at it with a wooden pencil;
I threw the beer down on the stone paving
Parched by the East Wind

Which sucked the infusion dry,
The wasp glued by its wings
To the fizzing stone.
I stamped on it,
Smeared its appearance across the paving
Like a drawing or a fossil;
'How could you have done it!'
Blood from her steak had stained her creamed potatoes;
'It was the East Wind,' I explained.

V

'The eager wasp that nips for its steak
Small stained loaves of the butcher's bloody sawdust,
That secateurs threads each autumn from my muslin
  shirt,
Each autumn nibbles from your Shakespeare . . .'

'If you had swallowed it . . .
It would have been like cutting your hand on the book,
Like swallowing the whole pepper-tree,
Like devouring the Undertaker's Wind.'

AT WESTMINSTER ABBEY

Chambered like a pomegranate, fragrance
Like the interior of a stone fruit;
The shrine of the six kings at the core
Of the mystery-building, where there is a small
Open chamber, pillared; behind the altar
In the dark the six kings lie.
From their tombs a distant reaching-out
Sensed, very weak, tendrils of non-visible mist
Charged with the grave like a medicine
Which is also poison, suggesting a riddle,
Or dust assembling a tongue in the tabernacle,
Very weird, very weak, like a signalled sexual
Certainty, but remote, as though the bones chimed
Very far away, and gave out a fragrance
Not quite liked, and the stomach sank,
In the core-chamber, with the six kings
Circling an abyss in which bones whirled,
Rose and fell. I said to the abyss
'Forgive me my sins,' it was all I could say
To that. To those kings. Who professed Christ.

STARLIGHT

Her menstruation has a most beautiful
Smell of warm ripe apples that are red,
And an odour of chocolate, a touch of poppy,
And bed-opiums roll from her limbs
Like the smokes of innumerable addicts between the sheets,

A morpheus tampon like a tomb of spices,
Full of spirits, red firework.

It makes me feel like Hercules!
Who spun the wheel in the house of women.
Indeed, the wheel spins, a crimson thread.
Suddenly, the stars are out,
Ripe, like the apples;
Menstruating, with the stars out.

THE PLACE

Are we mad because of the place, or is it
A mad place because we are lunatic
In Cornwall's biggest open-air
Mental hospital with the name of a town,
And the appearance of a Town
And many visitors who profess themselves refreshed
And sleep well in Bedlam. I have a book
Which says that Falmouth 'possesses the most
Relaxing climate in the United Looniebin'
And I believe it, because our tourists
Stroll with wide-open eyes along the sleepy paths
Seeing one of the matters mostly difficult
That invisibly surround us like accustomed dreams:

Here, Thunder is inaudible King; we are
In continual audience, he is crowned
With cumulo-nimbus and electricity and
He likes coronation so much he does it ten times daily;
You cannot quite hear his vivat, but his rumbling
Passes away under our feet and the moon hangs
Among his vapour-ranges trembling like a gong
And the great oyster-bed shines with phosphor brine
The energy of its pearl-making in the depths,
Each one must have a full-moon in its chalk box just like that,
The queen oyster made of white satin soft as phlegm,
Every shell a queen;

The King passes into the water,
The Queens tempt him
With heads that open, displaying pearls.

DESSERT

I

Sherbet, sweet snow, exact flipside
Of parching desert sand, it slinks
Into the warm puddle of the mouth
And fizzes there like a shock of rain
And makes the palate spin
Tented veils of water in its oasis; desert fruitjuice,
Scented rain stiffened with sugar, and packed back
Into its fruitskin; so bodies
Plump their clothes and shine from their openings
Like stars through mothy clouds. Unfolding
Our silken sleeping-sacks we slither
Into fluttering dreams.

II

The air pours over the English trees
Like green weirs and waterfalls. She dons
A certain silk with folded openings, her blouse;
It is like slipping on a thin
Indian temple, a sheath
Sculptured with erotic poses, very slender
And in constant twist, so our
Mouth parches, and we need kisses,
And sherbet of the oasis.

THE LONG VATICANS

The yachts purling past the blue headlands
Of bluebell woods, those flowers that root through
Like precious ore and vein of sapphire, the hill
Of blue-green horse that is resting with its sides
Gently heaving, shot through with a pulse of veins,
Veins of raw sapphire.

The resting Fal, the replete hills, the sated hills.

The water glares like a stretched sheet
The ferryboat is made of mist
It has a freight of souls travelling by their own light,
The wharf bolted to its shadow in the mirror
Great Christmas trees launched on the water
Which for lights are freighted
With soul upon soul.

Dawn: the hills wet shaggy shapes, newborn
With the waters winding between rapidly,
The hills conched, the horse-look got up and gone.
Night again: the working boats hardly scratch
The water which takes no permanent mark and settles
Into its sheet, then into its mirror, but now

All the drowned sailors rise over the hill
As one mighty constellation called 'Jack Starr'
With his dog snapping at his heel,
Mighty voyageur, mighty swaggerer;

Now the stars rise beneath our feet and above too,
They are everywhere at once,

The houses, the earthly stars
Blaze like furnaces, or well-heads
To subterranean light, the town
Is a mineral outcrop of radiant ores
Of clumped crystal-light in facets
As the stars pearl past in their yacht formations;

What if the damned turned into stars as well? They don't.
The moon rises over the long vaticans of the hills
Like a white pope laying open her churches.
I trace the wailing wind to its source; it is the moon.

As our child was conceived, a fresh wind blew
From those roots of granite
And the yachts purled between the hills;
It gave the sea visible pleasure to be sailed upon;
The clouds above were like dancers
Made of cathedral and horse, shot through with
Whiter veins, great blackwhite clouds
Like an unprinted bible, the scripture
Falling open like a rain of conception.

RAIN ON VAUX HILL

Everything flies open just for the child.
The book she opens is 200 magic mirrors,
Her bath gives her veridical knowledge of the oceans,
The living fire discloses battlefields fitfully lit,
Wagons burning, blood burning like wagon-grease,
Her dreaming head is like a great pearl,
Her paper kite a risen ghost, I attempt to grasp
How such a one feels about the rain, and about
The flying kites on Vaux Hill.

She runs off
Flying her kite, those people on the hill
Dip with their kites into the wet bread of clouds,
And the mass of electricity reaches down
With fingers of rain, lightning
Slips down the string, all the clothes shine.

Rain, rain, says the child, as one might say
Love, possible Love. Now the sun comes out,
The strong spirit that forces up the heaven
Like a great blue crust of bread.

Is it that the rain falls and the people's clothes
Become one cloth covering all, like a dream of bed
And everyone belonging to the same house
Which would be after they, we all are dead,
So the rain is a ghostly wireless catching voices,
Music, an extra weave into the skin?

They are now wet receivers and transmitters
Creating a certain perfume with the trees
And the kites flying in the rain on Vaux Hill:
See! the kite like a paper ghost
Or a spirit rising from the grave in its paper coffin
On the big shelving winds around Vaux Hill.

She will not discuss the matter any further.
She stood listening to me, clearly I was one
For whom the rain had no or little meaning,
It was not like electricity or wet bread,
Or paper ghosts, or sweets, or church,
Everybody in bed was near to it but not the same . . .
But what about
The adults on the hill? Ah, she said,
They were flying their kites as she was, and

As she said this there was a fresh
Rain-smell in her breath, closer
Than any words we had used, a new phrase,
And she laughed, and that was closer, the church was raining
And the chapel was a paper kite full of ghosts
The colour of summer showers and rain-smelling people,
But the mention of church destroyed it, she ran off.

THE STRANGER MINER

I note the wicker dome capping the mine-shaft,
The Dome of Serpents over the Pit
Of the Dead Man, in the local language.
The godless woman comes to her father with a troubled face,
She needs a draught from his vessels of force,
His categorical ideas, for she loves a miner.
The air is blue down there because of the malachite walls,
Sky underground, its metal is copper, and its perfume
Brass, which by custom comes close to cedar.
He takes her by the hand to see
The sweet low-browed Hathor he carved on a sea-cave wall,
Done in his minute scribing hand, the antidote
To the vibratory dynamite and the pick's creation
Of rubble of automobiles and galvanised cans -
To write a wonder-world underground
In the exhausted tunnels that are of no use
For anything but mysteries. It was his wet dream
To travel into the earth all work done
With a light on the brow of his cap
And a sculptor's bag in his hand; the gross delver
Expands and becomes the fine worker with a lighted brow
Who drives towards the thrones underground,
And these tunnels are as the outer folds of the garment
For in that inward part is the deep mystery
Of the Self-glittering One, who needs
No light on his cap. Worship therefore
The underground splash of ore for its beauty and not its use
And behold my light shed through these rocks,
I am a star which goes with thee and shines out of the depths
For man and wife ought to be garments the one to the other
And it is my delight to be thy garment. At that
He lifted his hand to his head and twisted the switch

And a total blindness descended. Though the air was still the
  same
And warm, it had become black; though she was the same self
And near him with his strange talk, and he was safe,
She was black, her clothes black, her flesh black,
And her black heart pumping black blood; she became aware
Of the perfumes of the rock spreading like a garden
That had never been seen, and there was a faint
Organ-tone that was the thud of the sea standing
In the corridors of stone, and it was black
Of a softness in which she could waft her hand, and
It was as though her eyes in straining towards the dark
Stretched like the horns of snails through softness
Until they hurt, and withdrew, and resting
There seemed to be faint lights, maybe through the rock
Of stars beyond rock, or maybe of his brainwaves
Closer by. 'What a strange miner you are,' she said,
'Please turn on the light,' 'Not so!' he said hotly
With a sudden lightning revealing himself
As though a furnace door had opened, with his hand
To the switch. 'Then whoever sees your mysteries
Buried in the soft-soot of ever-darkness?' 'That darkness
Has its eyes, and the sweet smells you sense I know
Were never here until I carved the walls by feeling only
Not in the light of my brow, or they were in ore-bud,
Now they are full-flowering.' So she went
For another draught from her father's cold vessels
Of categorical ideas. He was left alone to question
What part of the mystery was in the night aboveground
In the windy wet street as she hurried home,
The big wet leaves blowing,
For when the day dawns, other stone flowers
Open underground, and are a light there,
And you may meet their perfumes
Pouring out of the mine-shafts and walking abroad
In tall shafts of sunlight, marrying with
The mist the trees make like an ultimate milk.

AT THE OLD FOLKS' HOME

The old folk cover their faces with the sandy newsprint
In the garden of the oak-shingled home in the lemon-grove.
When he saw his granddaughter coming towards him
He gave her a quick squirt of ignore-me gas from his deckchair,

But it did not diminish his visibility as he had hoped
And she came on in a straight line.

The child with her and the two dogs
Prowling at her heels suddenly looked
Like ruthless old men. Dogs and children
Are mirrors of meat and blood as they grow up, but
Was I that ruthless?

She sat down and started talking about their zoo-visit,
Frankly and in the presence of the child
Describing the camels fornicating behind the rocks,
Concerning herself with the lion and his right-angled bent prick
Pissing golden rain all over the visitors through the bars
With his lordly back turned; they were not expecting this, looked pleased.

And her talk ranged ever-deeper into the past:
The book kiosk, where she worked with other plump women
Dressed in beige cardigans; and the woman whose kimono
Caught fire while she was masturbating.

He stopped the flow of talk: let's have a beer,
It is the prime brand of bottled Falmouth,
Drink it by the neck; you mean toast
The future king and queen, she cried, and he agreed.

CARCASS

In the bellies of the soft bronze flies
The carcass of the magpie flies again,
Humming like a fast song,
A gong hushed but purring to the touch.
The aviary of insects chirps with juice
They are working with their faces
At the white branches of the carcass,
Pungent little resurrectors, pepper-fruit
In bronze of false orchards slipping away
Full of their pips in lariat flight,
The magpie flies again
Through the churches of the air,
It breaks its dome
Laid by a fly in a black-white flurry,
The reverse stork that devours eggs and nestlings
Wings backwards down the gullets of resurrectors.

The navvy bows his head to the freezing asphalt,
His pneumatic thumper pounds the road
Belling with the decelerated fury
Of the wellington-boot tongue
Of a blowfly on its pitons hacking like a hero
Hard at a slab of refrigerated giant.

RACKMASTER

The perfumed torturers,
The rackmaster's crew: everywhere
He has turned himself and his minions
Into perfect machinery
For torturing at a distance;
It was not torture when the reaper
Addressed his field with his single blade:
That was willing sacrifice, and the wheat bent to the steel
As the steel-grey head of the man bent to his reaper,
For in that harvest the reaper would fall.

Now I see a mechanical castle or high chariot
Moving slowly over the ripe wheatfield
Harvesting it as a war machine harvests soldiers,
In the chalky layers of fog
A castle moving with its blades over the ripe fields,
The rackmaster's crew lodged in its bowels,
The air full of wheat-dust in its wake,
A ship of the wheat, harvesting the waves;

I have looked down into the atomic reactor,
Into its swimming-pool where nobody can bathe,
And I have seen leaking from its elements the blue of
  unclouded sky,
Matter pulled apart in this well to release sky,
Matter tortured in a well, and now it tortures us.

ROUND PYLONS

The clouds of luminous mist from the sea
Laying the round dew everywhere in the hedges
And the coils of innumerable dew encircling the spider,

The circuitry of the brash spider
In round pylons
As in a castle of awareness,

Many curtain walls and cistern keeps
Guarding the centre
And, down its lines of gossamer

The round helmets of light
In their slow march,
The land hung with these sheets,

The sheeted sea coming ashore
And hanging its pictures up in the hedges,
Its unsalted portraits,

The surface of the sea doubling
As it opens into sleep,
A source among white sources, cresting.

SAILING THROUGH

With a pick and shovel and aching arms
He unearths the fossil of galleon
Under the greenhouse floor
With rotten poop and forecastle just standing and whole-nave
ribs.

Even before the excavations searched
Under the spanking greenhouses with their sparking panes
Like see-through sails, even before
He acknowledged the creaking of their frames like tackle,
And before the perfume of soft fruit under glass had got
That tough ozonous tang to it like riven seas,
And before the white crests of the blossoms rhymed
With surfing waves, he had paused and leaned
On his spade and listened to the notes
Of a ship's bell chiming under the rich earth.

It was this note that set him
To burrow through his soft beds
Uprooting his precious blackberries, his pennants of red-
currants:
The very path
That led up to the glazed warm doors
Walked the plank above the buried jib-boom,
And the vigorous fruct and root
Of his intertwining horticulture had crammed
The subterranean hull – that had been
Its cargo, with the rudder itself
Wedged under the house and laid bare
By delving up the cellar.

Now he knows how his garden sails, he will take
Immense plaster-casts of the whole vessel

And present it to the museum like a white ghost-ship;

After, all he has dug up he will replace,
Including the chest of gold uncovered
In the ship's waist, below his famous blackcurrants
And piratical redcurrants, to sail on ringing
Its underland bell, docking its visible soft-fruit treasure-cargo.

EXPEDITION

Under a Sorcerer's Moon, a Way Place
Where the two worlds touch and cross
As two perfumes interpenetrate, Hardy
Disappeared down the ventilation shaft
With an orgasmic cry. We found him
With our torches and rescued him
From the cold spring water, we drank
His health, we massaged his feet
In the lather of medicinal soap
And cave spring. He put his hand
Up to the web of dressings.

There were two torchbearers
Drinking in the cavern, whose lights
Made a white lodge surrounded
With nourishing blackness, they finished
And began beating the surface of the dark lake
With paddles; it was black theatre,
The cave seemed empty but we knew it was full,
The lights shone full into our eyes
And the rock was draped with thick black moss
Underfoot as well as on the walls, we knew
The performers dressed in black had assembled
Because the darkness breathed; then, very slowly,
Mailed fish, large sandstone slabs printed
With archaic skeletons, quartz crystals
The size of footballs entered floating
From the arched recesses, fluttering and looking
For a stopping-place. 'Take my head!'
Yelled Hardy, 'And give me instead
One of those inspired stones that crease
The light, and even in darkness are
Sounding chambers for drapery of radio . . . '

Immediately chords burst out
Overhead and underneath our feet, so that
We saw we were just so enclosed
In a cavern of quartz, the moss transparent
Like forests of glass, the water
Bright as milk, and Hardy with a head
Full of light slowly beating like inner wings, and crying
'May everybody have at length a head like mine!'
We had to put his head in a sack to bring him out of the mine.

THROUGH THE GOAT CURTAINS

(country pub)

'It is physiolatry,' he muses,
Sipping his drink and weaving a red shroud
Out of wine. In this place, pool
Or uterus of the pub garden
He catches the whole breath of the sun,
The emaning mouth. There is a pigeon made of gold
While it stands in the sunbeam; the entrance
To this little rocky garden with the well
Was covered over with curtains that appeared
To be woven of goat's hair. There are no tombs
In this church, no old blind men
Turning into worms, only
Gently settling and fermenting tuns. He stayed there
Reading his drink until the stars came out,
Above him the pole star on which all turns
In the declared map of the heavens. Dew
Condensed over the cool metal table
Like a planisphere with a hole at the centre
For an umbrella-pole, dew
In its own constellations. One drink
And he has seen all the stars, above and below.
Well-satisfied, he pushes his way
Back through the musty goat's hair curtains to the bar.

TRAIN TO READING

The tide is perhaps
Librarian of the game,
Pulling out and pushing back
The new books of water;
There are crisp frills and buttons,
Beaches of buttons;
It is as some explosives
Produce heat and no gas, for example
Silver acetylide, which explodes
To soot and powdered silver;
The lights in the wavelets
Like piles of silver coins
Shivering and exploding
To nothing but new selves, and heat.
A pat of greenfly
Soldered to the front of the engine
Of the Penzance-Reading express,
A tunnel scooped out of summer insects,
Our journey pressed to a button;
The librarian buttons
At your neck flash and strain
Like silver explosives,
It is as the librarian stacks
The chinking waves at her own speed
And the insects explode
The corpse into glory; together
We board the insect-murdering express;
In the firelight the ceiling
Bumps up and down
Like the lid of a box;
We explode together
Producing great heat
And fall apart once more
As you and I.

WOODEN PIPES

The hands in the womb,
The invisible hands serving at the feast,
The round banquet in the high domed hall,
Shaping the child and serving her,
Combing her body to the right shape;
This is going on now.

I believed I heard Zoe
Playing on wooden pipes as plain as plain
But as I woke fully
It was a seagull crying.

There is an inner, and an outer daughter.

My sleep makes me as my waking does,
The sleep of invisible hands
Of servitors, the music of wooden pipes,
The tree-song shortened for human ears,
The blessed ghosts of that feast
And the drunken guest at it, the reveller
Who wakes in the cold air
To the music of seagulls.

There is an inward, and an outer daughter,
And the outer girl sits, combing her hair,
The mother watching, takes the comb
Soothes her head, gliding out of it
Aches of the day with her visible hands,

For with invisible hands the same woman
Below and within is combing
Another daughter into shape
Among the birth-currents
A womb of full tresses

And the outer daughter speaks to the inner
Through the mother,
The inner daughter speaks through the mother's actions,
The two sisters are combing each other's hair,
The mother is the interface,
The two daughters kiss her.

THE RIDERS

We await the opal miner, the miner of moonstone.
The glasses attend us like counsellors who
Are black cats also, for the dark beer purrs
With the bubbles of its soft white muzzle;
It will make its leap through the hoop
Of the gullet and coil red in the paunch
Under the great leather belt creaking like rafters.

We, the people in the bar, will not take a drink
Until the later-joiner cometh; he is
That one man standing in the bows of the shallop
Intently watching the rower of him across
The water dark as beer with its foaming moon-path.
The conference will be both drunk and sober.
We might agree to one drink, now he doth come,
The glassy skeletons of the counsellors collected
And their black flesh renewed, which is to say
Filled with gods, and the late-comer our Brewer
Who knows how to drink. We regard

Those larval god-images of the counsellors
Whose eloquence uncoils through every gut,
The gods who worm through guts making speeches;
It is thus they appear. The shallop grinding gravel,
The light foot-step landing, the door
Pushed open, we offer him his glass
And we all drain ours and wipe our lips
And smile at the fire, and then at him.

He opens his soft leather pouch and throws across
The great wooden bar made from a single tree
The shining moonstones, the pale-rainbowed opals.
It is as he promised. The stones are here.

I look at the stelled glistening, it has arranged
Its pattern in which I think I see
A horse with wings, and its rider. 'Shall we call
This house *The Ridered Horse*?' is my suggestion.
They all stare down: 'My pattern is a Snake . . .'
'. . . Mine a Dolphin . . .' – 'But they all have Riders,
Do they not?' declares the Brewer, 'We must
Call ourselves The Riders.' The bar
Looked as though an opal piece of sky had dropped
And burst in constellations. 'Where are those mines?'
I asked myself as I watched the Moon rise
Into the leaded panes and the scattered stones
Across the deeply-polished wood answered them.

ZOE'S THOMAS

A young leggy cat, so glossy black
He might in that instant have leapt
From the pitch-egg of night; his eyes

Golden as yolks. He scrutinizes
The room-dew of our breath running down
The cold windowpane as if it were mice.

A cluster of drops scuds down the glass
And shatters on the sill, his paw darts out
And inquisitorially turns the meagre

Water over and over - and then his tongue
Darts out and swiftly laps it up,
The innocent water which squeals with light.

MY DOG

I sheared my mongrel dog
And used his white coat in plaster.
All my ceilings were strengthened with my dog's coat.

The elm outside roars like a mill-wheel.
I have gathered for insulation
Shells from the beach to lay between my rafters.

My ceilings hiss like a beach when the wind blows,
Howling at the moon. I sit in the new house
As one might sit in the new moon, waxing.

I watch the small brown spider
Wax his clean wheel. He sits at the centre
Of his attention like a gondola

Of an airy ship, or like a ready
Small boat with copper oars
Which rows a cargo of syrup,

An Aethyr ship tasting of radar and moths.

HIGHTOWN

Where the churches like stone sleepers
Sit bolt upright in bed,
And where sleepers like crucifixes are laid
Each night gently in the feathery beds,
One dream is that the ceiling is cobbled;
This signifies hail.
After the rainbows conceived by sunshine and hail,
Howling winds strip off the robe of the promise,
And each house is a church this Whitsun
For all the home crucifixes sprout bed-feathers
And storm into the night -

In the night each home sends its petrels into the storm,
Dreamers alight on the coigns and howling vantages
Preening and cleaning themselves
Of the blood which is the yolk of the human egg;

They may ascend when they have completed this task,
On their white pinions, if they are able.

Sleepless I open my curtain
I look deep into the eyes of a seabird alighted on my sill,
I look into the gold vessels which are like church plate
Mounted in the lens-liquids of the eyes,
For this lordly-necked sea-voyager sees through holy utensils,
And the humans put on the cross, putting their wings on
By which they ascend, and the robe of the promise falls about
them
Now that the wind has dropped, and rainbows are possible
again
And moonbows among the heavens of bright electricity in the
frosty morning.

The dawning rooms of our homes are lighted by like means,
With waterfalls of electricity
Resembling those the dreamer explores,
And in his robes of ascension wears;
It issues in small bottled fountains of shining wire,
And torrents of electricity pour into our eyes
Which come from the watery mountains
Scraping against the sky
And fall into our eyes which are communion-plate and dish antennae;

Thus fire enters water, as the radio of light,
And I click off at the door my fountain of current
That shines off the white ceilings which are smooth,
For now the sky is losing its white ceiling,
And snow with its snap lights the whole ground;
The sky divests itself in feathers,
Full of sheer blue electricity instead.

QUIET TIME

The spider of the wainscot
Fell to the pliers newly arrived
Of a centipede out of the WC pedestal;
This aggressor was like the last bones of a God
Waiting for resurrection of the whole body,
Like an Osiris pillar, a small one,
A small god's spinal column
Running independently, as a God's might do –

But also like a long twist of toffee
Of that colour as I sat remembering
When toffee was the gold of my boy's mouth,
And would not pluck the fillings from my teeth;
And this long twisted toffee has its own jaws
With which it strikes down the defenceless weaver
I have watched patching his sail
For several days in this same cloistered toilet –

My quiet time; a cloister's clyster, that centipede
Is like a dark cloister running on its own
That has loosened itself from the Abbey stones
Incorporating into its twilight many brethren
Sprinting all together on brotherly legs
Like Chinese masquers chattering in their dragon –

Hunting for all the tremulous spinsters
And all the lockchesters in the world,
Hunting for the alchemistic spiders
For they have within them a Benedictine
Stilled from the swarms of prayerful night-moths
One of which now splashes the cream walls
Easing the fretted constellations of its cream wings;
I thought it was a speckling of ink, like –

DOMESTIC SUITE

The central heating buzzes
Like an apple with a wasp inside;
Water-tree-house with a bark of copper,
The taps flower white water,
Dribble glass moss.
Outside the sea spreads tablecloths over and over,
Is full of milt,
The strong pure eggs of fish;
In the shops the pure pleated eyes of fish,
Salty goldfoil, open to all their troubles.
I slice the orange; it is a round table
Its place-segments designed for knights,
Fitted with sealed goblets of juice as for astronauts.
Our hen squeaks like a wooden sash.
The shore breathes like a horse
Running under the shade of trees into the sunlight,
In this wind, white horses or blossoming trees rush inland.
The meadow-breathing of a pony, the strong
Leathery lips as they nip up the sugar-lump,
The strong warm grassy flank;
There is the central heating with its low pulse,
There is golden foliage and a glittering wife, there is
An unweaned child that smells of honeysuckle in the nights,
and
Subdued water-music of horses and wasps all winter.

OPULENT

The black mirrors of the slate stairs
Of the quarry, opulent with the rain,
Pouring with white curtains,
And the unexpected, permanent perfumes of rock,
Opulent. The lamp turned up
Through which the air travels so sweetly,
Mineral oil, odour of rock. Sound of rock,
The stone chimes hanging in the window; flowers
Red as rust in the rain
On the lip of the old mine
And I move to the open shaft
To inhale the deep breath
Out of the lungs of this mine. The cathedral
Of the horse's face marked out in the cliff
Modelled by the sea, horse-like, galloping,
Cliff eyes sealed shut, two shafting nostrils
Dipped into the surf, foam-breathing. The seawind
Gusting through the houses, rattling
Knife-drawers and door-knobs and
Misting mirrors, the sky full of gulls
Rising like a champagne of winged bubbles
Over the two streams marrying at the hill's foot.
I am startled by a dozen brown ducks like one
Panicky brown spider sprinting free under the giant
Rhubarb-leaves, green transoms; the rain
Has fallen one hour, the world breathes
Expected impermanent scents
That the blind man may see beyond sight for one hour,
Opulent without eyes.

IN THE NEW FOREST

They march away like pillars of Woodhenge,
The narrowing glooms between the Douglas firs, the perfumed
glooms;
The silver larch-boles like hammered moonbeams

Whispering in the sky; the larch-part
Of the forest in moonlight, always;
The tarantula'd forest - for at the butterfly-farm

In a sandy vivarium among the indigenous jungle
Where the blooms beat their wings, and hover,
Bloom settling on bloom, and entering, a spider's

Empty statue with a trapdoor open wide
In its husky back from which it has
Given birth to itself in a tender beige

Fist-sized, with fingers, and hardening
From helplessness in the coddling shadow, unhusked
In the balsamic foot-square desert, enspiders

Those firs, who litter, unhusking their needles
Slipping layer on layer exacting a fragrance
Which is the front end of eternal, for time slows down

Among the moon-coloured boles, the scaly pines;
Dehisced nuts, and twigs that are small boughs,
Litter on a descending scale of all the tree does,

Fronding wisps of all the herbs and all the shrubs
Sliding over a black soil under it,
Made of it. As the rain falls on this dust it composes

A mighty odour of forest-soul; I will take some home
In a match-box, and wet it when I need to return.
Perfume the sixth state of matter

Clambering into its web-centre. Then on
In the sunset to visit the Rufus-stone.

THE DYNAMITE DOCTORS

The dynamite doctors
At the explosives factory
They nurse the melted stew

Like greasy gravy or mutton tallow,
A grey potency in its bowls
That must never be stirred too fast

Or else the door opens on a star
Opens on a sun, on creation
And the fire-blast hurries in

Like an angel of death with hair burning.
The ticklish doctors
Skimming the bowls

Tilting them over the kieselguhr
To contrive that virile mud
Called dynamite,

The precious stream that must not break
In its droplets like a stick of bombs,
Otherwise the medicine will suffer an attack

Which will take everyone with it.
One doctor takes the pulse
Of the machine and turns it down

A little, the vibration is excessive;
He dips his finger slowly
Into the gluten and sucks it most gently

So his head shall not explode:
He nods, he must not shake his head.

A WORLD

The world full of sugar and rain
Rubs up against us with its muzzles.
The hanging lamps of convolvulus
Shedding scent like radiance, like
Reading-lamps of black light
That is perfume, the snail
Fastened to the stem reads its scroll
From inside, with black light.
The wooden click or tock
As the fertile cone drops, the wood
Ticking like a wooden clock
As the timber roses drop,
The cogged pine-cones
Full of yellow honey and
Cough-drop gums, lung-healing balsams
In the wet pine-forest smelling like a
Healing sickroom, some gigantic person
Recovers himself among balsamic odours
And white sheets of water; I can see
With rinsed, convalescent eyes
As the odours roll down the vistas
Like gigantic nurses in headdresses;

The tree shedding its mirror down its trunk,
Glistening balsams, where the big-bummed aphids
Feed like drops of the fat river, like tuns,
Like cisterns brimming with green medicines,
Like articulated tankers transporting green serums,

Or Aesculapian galleys rowing with many legs,
Or stout pots of herbal tea,
Their eyelash-legs finer than razor cuts,
The sap of a wounded tree still walking,
The portly Green Man in an insect mask.

MENOPAUSA

The change of life in her
Was like the escape of an animal,
Escape of a lizard maybe, like a fast
Comma escaping the sentence and jumbling it;
Like buildings where the main beam snaps,
The broken floors and the rubble descending
In their clouds of pepper. I will build

A new hall of statement, she said; I am tired
Of all this blood. It was the lizard
Which had wounded her, and lodged,
That now departed. She pointed
To the Moon rising, and the man in it
And said: there he is, my lizard,
Sailing away.

Or was it the woman had escaped
And offered her shadow to the dark gods?

Shadow or lizard, both slipped quickly
Like silk over the ground,
Would swerve and misdirect and disappear;

And often it seemed
As if she herself had gone
And the lizard remained,
The dry sand of the lizard
Pouring. For she
Could sit long minutes not stirring,
The eyes blinking

Seldom; then she would reach out
For an apple with an arm so graceful
It seemed a tongue; and a film

Wiped across her eyes as if to cleanse them,
A second eyelid, and then the film departed
And the eyes sparkled like gems in dry sand;

If it were a lizard, it was a seer,
Like a sphinx; after these reveries,
Munching apples, she would write long poems
To her friends, each one enclosing a letter.

MY HEART

When my heart came to me in my hand, I thought:
Your body is a temple, and you
Are the master in it. Was I, hell!
The bookshop down the blind alley,
At the end of the rainy alley smelling
Of prams and paving-stones, it is as though
It were selling me my own books back,
For it has many of the books I bought years back,
But I am in love with the assistant, and this means
I have twice over the books I already have.
She is an American; she can sell me

Anything. She took my cigarette from my hand
(The hand my heart came to me in) and started
Smoking it with a direct look through the grey smoke.
Her eyes were of the same colour as the smoke,
She held up a grey book against her chest,
I saw she wore a grey opal; a low cry
Draws my attention to the crib in the corner
Folded with grey blankets among the piles of books
Tight-shut as oyster-beds. The opal and the baby,
The baby and the opal and the books, the woman
In a grey cloud of cigarette smoke worn
Like a mask fading off her direct look, the soft light
Dwelling in the grey pages she closed up,
Dwelling in all the pages of this bookshop, as it might;
But I would have to buy the shop to find that out.

THE DOCTOR RETURNS

A meeting specified in the Glazier's Arms
By Dr Fu-Manchu, that Sunday lunchtime
Its busiest hours, I did not see

How we could discuss our private
And criminal business in that place,
But when I arrived, I understood. Gone

Were the stockbroker tweeds and the
Brassy-haired wives, the colonel's ice-cold
Clipped moustache and the twinsets. The bar

Was totally full of the Doctor's sinister cohorts.
Here were his wide-shouldered stocky dacoits
In their clean blue uniforms like mechanics on duty;

There were several Chinese of high rank, with coral beads
Pimpling their mandarin caps, who with delicacy lifted
Small sherries in hands that were ivory cages

Of long twisted fingernails; sitting on the bar
I saw three black pigmies being treated
To Babychams; they had left their blowpipes

Stuck in the walking-stick stand which was a shellcase;
And there were several distinguished-looking Englishmen
In the snowy coats of scientists whom I knew

By their glazed eyes were under the fluence
Of Fu-Manchu's famous toadstool distillates;
Then silence fell.

The Doctor was near. We felt it. He came
In through the swing door in an overcoat
With an astrakhan collar, he was taller

And thinner than any of us as he walked
Up to the bar, his green eyes veiled
By their membranes like a bird of prey

His face of Satan and his Shakespearean brow
Striking a notable chill; and ordered, sibilating,
A double chartreuse the colour of his eyes, with ice.

WHITE MIDAS

It is the Pope, the veritable white Polish Pope,
The Pope who has been a poet, the published Pope,
He who kisses the soil, and accordingly

Worships a Black Virgin, now like a Christ-child
He has re-arrived, in a cradle, a deep wicker,
And it has a glow of dayspring gold, an aura,

As though he were frying delighted in pure oil:
He was vibrating gold and this was his atmosphere,
And I? I was tending him

Like a secret ornament . . . even
Such a being must change nappies
But they were scalding-hot, and I

Could not touch them. I looked closer,
I saw it was not piss had made them heavy –
They were woven gold, gold spun and braided.

ENTRY FEE

When I stroke her arms
There is a smell of bread;
Her legs, of lilies.

There are fragrant marshes in her skin
And there is a pulse in the ground of it.
The Mine called 'Isyours' is open today
On payment of a small compliment.

This is really
Very extraordinary value;
The lights are blazing underground,
Gemstones stud the walls and floors;
I walk there amazed for hours, it seems.

At the very bottom of the shaft
There is a dark pool with a white swan floating

It rouses its wings

It beats over the water
Pleating it to its depths
Raising a new odour charged
With the deep and with the extreme
Cry of the bird as it ladders across the pool.

DR BACH'S FUGUE

(Edward Bach, already a distinguished physician, is reputed to have discovered the remarkable homoeopathic remedies known by his name, by running wild in the woods and fields like a Merlin.)

The Bach flight, the fugue,
The Bach traces
Like an atmosphere labyrinth,
The green healers
That wave their branches in the air
Diffusing medicine.
Edward Bach, physician,
Tore his waistcoat open,
Ran mad in the woods
Like a wildman Merlin,
And thus in depression
(The strong man fighting himself)
Found relief shaking dew
From leaves of *Oak*,
One gulp from the tree
He was well, and stood up again
Under its canopies,

Yet he remained hopeless -
Very great hopelessness -
And *Whin*, the common furze,
Offered him its hypodermic dews
Caught on its every point;
Yet he was still shaken
By mental arguments,
So the Lord *Horse Chestnut*
Trembled rain upon his bowed head;
He was proud still

And scooped *Water-violet*
Out of its lowly duck-pond
To aid him in that;
Still he was in fear and trembling
So *Mimulus* succoured,
The capering Monkey-Flower,
And he strolled off whistling,
But this hid black worry
And *Agrimony* offered
Fallen blooms scudding a puddle
And the next layer peeled off
For he ran in a panic,
The flower god
Piped everywhere,
He snatched up
The trailing *Rock-rose*
Which melted in his mouth
And he swallowed his terror
Which had kept him running,
So now, stock still, without will
Turned to stone, he just
Manages to stir to pluck
Centaury, and it melts his bonds
Which are all his degrees
And they scatter like a necklace snapped
And he is indecisive
Whether to return to the consulting rooms
And exchange black-trousered opinions
From which uncertainty
The tiny flowers
Of the annual *Knawel*
Rescue him
And bring him to the *Wild Oat*
In its fatherly fields - he samples
And immediately becomes over-critical . . .

Rubbed over his face,
The azure *Chicory*, tall plant,
Resolves his mind,
So in his enthusiasm
He has to take *Vervain*
Which makes him day-dreamy,
For which *Clematis* suffices -
But then he feels lonely,
And *Heather* is specific,
Though after
He could not trust himself:
Here, *Plumbago* is sovereign,

And for the doubt, *Gentian*.

Now he is exhausted
Olive comes to him,
And as his strength rises
Vine soothes him,
And being to himself
A hard master to the last,
Rock Water slakes his thirst.

NEGOTIUM PERAMBULANS...

If they can get across our garden they have eaten it,
Feeding off flowerfaces, creaming the innocent smiles,
Blooms disclosing tall heaven, each a feretory,
Subject to the rasps of ambulant grey-mackintosh pillows.

How I wish our garden were infested with swans!
Like serpent angels with white wings that thunder
And shout with power that is white and of all colours,
Swan like an electrical dream about a snake in my pillow.

The slug's movement is that of a bad snake made of plastic
Awarded artificial motion by an unnatural scientist
Who slips one under the head of all our flowers;
The pillow eats the head in the dreamy garden.
So I have employed a slug-danseuse to rid us of them;
She has occupied the garden hut with the balsam of her unwashed
Ghostteeshirts drenched with gymnastic meditations;
She fires a little pistol into the swarming bees to show me
The speed of some people's percipience; see,
None falls, none is shot, this gives me confidence;
She dances like a foetus twitching and they're gone.

(Whereas the polluted cities have unclean frost,
Filthy vernix, greasy as a dead-face,
Here we have thunderstorms and awe-inspiring slugs
Which are bigger than a human eye, swallowing the garden.)

THE ALTAR

I woke with a start at dawn, painted
On the inside of my eyelids a vivid flash
Of the old monument buried in bushes at the lawn's end,
The black monument, belly-height; I was filled
With the idea of scrubbing it until it shone
Gold, as sandstone should, like the Whitehall
Ministries once more emerging from their scaffolds
Where they had rained with sprays for months,
The golden walls disclosed behind the dripping tarpaulins.
I took two scrubbing-brushes. One
For the first work and a new brush
For the final touches, creaking over my arm
A bucket of warm water, detergent, and a pair of secateurs.
As I freed the altar from its entangling brambles
The mist hung from branches like torn-up
Letters of the alphabet. The soot came off
Immediately in jet-black foam. Around me
Was space, spontaneous light, the soft cold
Grayling dawn, purely cloud and delicacy of matter.
Now the hulking stone revealed its delicacy,
Its guilloche carvings snaking among stone leaves
And branches on the four sides; but on the flat top
I had uncovered a plate set flush that as I scrubbed
Shone, bright steel; I noticed in one corner
A tiny inscription graved; 'They spill their blood in fear
On the altar of the sword-blade; let the only sacrifice
Be to the Lord.' The altar I had cleaned was made
Of sandstone and swordblades, gold and silver, the garden-
  leaves
Shifting like autumn multitudes in its mirror.

MARRIAGE CONTINUED

I wake up in your body. The talking
Bed, the mountains like a fleecy
Breath, the sky queerly lustred

By an indistinct sun. I wake up
Inside you, as it is the marriage today.
We must withdraw, and dress.

For a bouquet, she holds
A small prayer-book in her gloved hands,
And she is pale with the prestige of the moment.

At her astonished, blissful smile,
Unexpected haloes appear in the greenery
Like winged gates. My groom's eyebrows

Suddenly become cross-hatched. Now I can wake up
Inside her every dawn. She has foliages
Of subliming odour between her legs; he

Shall come down unto her
Like the rain into a fleece of wool.

AT HOME

I

The spider combs her beard.
One gave me cobweb-pills for the shakes.
There is a black Rasputin-fly that can't be killed,

There is a dustbin boiling with its worms;
My mother scrapes more porridge into the faces.
The flies buzz with swollen lips,

In a Russian, in the translating sunshine.
Dew scuttles down the panes
Like the shaky ghosts of crippled spiders.

I try to rub the glass free and clear
But they are running their races
On the further surfaces. The dry spider

Will raise the wet flies and drink out of them,
Like Bellarmine jugs, like horny flasks
That have wings and faces. Convolvulus

That smells of nice blancmange
Twirls about the dustbin lattice.
My father rushes through the kitchen

Flapping a tea-towel, ushering a ghost of flies
Out of the kitchen into the cool green lane.
There are still flies that circle stolidly

Keeping the pattern just below the ceiling.
They pass through my father's cloth, evidently,
Like spirits of the pattern. He returns.

II

He returns wiping his brow spiderous with dew
And breathing heavily. He shakes his fist
At the immovable fly-pattern round and round the lamp;

My father hefts a shuddering pail of water
And turns it into milk with disinfectant.
He pours it in the choiring bin of maggots.

Their smell of coconut and pus
Fades behind the blanket of hospital pine.
The maggots skip in their stringy boiling.

My mother folds her arms and nods her head.
We settle once more round the breakfast-table,
There is a baby brother hoisted in a high-chair.

The silent changeling grasps the shaggy rusk.
He was born in a smell of pine-needles and maggots.
I was not allowed inside the curtained room.

Its shadows were odorous, and deeper than a cave.
The doctor brisked the taps to scrub his paws.
He smelled of her, and the nurse smelled;

Pine and maggots. In the cave of bedroom shade
Where she has gone, her voice deepens like a man's
Then shatters, and another voice

Lifts in something which is not a song,
And she returns,
Gripping a maggoty bundle, not the same.

III

This terrible head suited her as well,
Distilling tears and wax and drool,
Lying across the pillow stained like brown paper,

Stamped and water-marked with sweat,
Just unwrapped, this parcel, on a fresh head,
The ginger hair in feeble ringlets,

The mauve lipstick, the broken veins in the cheeks,
Severed at the seamy sheet. It
Begins tossing, lets out an accustomed cry;

I start back, and clamber under the bed.
Here there are long lattices of dust
Rolled up against the wainscot from the blankets,

Fibres minutely ground through the springs
That coil above me, the mill
Of nightmare sickness and copulation,

The flour of germs and fibres rubbed
From bar and dance-hall all loafed together
In long limbless clooties which drift at me,

Shift very slightly in the mattress-wind
That puffs as she turns over in her sleep
Of the medicine alcohols that net her dreams

Blackening in the broken veins
Exhaling tinctures into the fresh window air
That begins again to smell of pine and coconut

And taint her appeaseless, helpless ghost.
It is in the boards and bricks.
The room and house will always smell of it.

JOY GORDON

The death of my mother, it
Doesn't mean she's gone for ever,
It means she has crossed over;
I cry because I have tears, and there seems to be
A joy in the air (she liked
To call herself Joy, it was her
Dancing name, Joy Gordon, thus,
When she danced she was my Father's Joy;
His name was Gordon.)

What are ghosts? The medium said
Whenever you think of her,
Greet that image kindly, say
'I'm glad to see you' it will give
The spirit Joy; to be fluxile
Like air, but
Constant as metal,
Not keeping to the one world,
Seeking unity with the living:
I see her now, she dances,
I am very glad to see you dancing,
Joy.

I see spirits, and try
To greet them kindly; and there is never
A company of the living
Without its spirits mingling:
There they were
Doing their Tai Chi
Under the dawn trees, the living
In their loose linen jackets and white ghost-trousers
A ballet of clowns moving as the trees move
To the dawn wind and the dawn chorus,

And among them, spirits,
Like air coiling, as though
Certain enhancing lenses had swept
In front of trees
Or between the dancers;

Under the dawn trees collecting
All the natural forces that do us good,
Gathering the metals of the trees
In manual alchemy, in sequent poses
Adopting the shapes of the vessels
Of human distillation, the hushed
Receptacles, and without, within,
The condensation of a magical dew;
To gather Joy.

The fair-haired one in the long skirt
A portion of the gnosis
Dancing slowly under the dawn trees,
She was the first one there, she was dancing
When I arrived, slowly under the dawn trees
To catch their bright metal, the distillation vessel
Itself dancing.

Just so might my daughter
Call herself Zoe Peters
For dancing or other joys
And signify 'Peter's Life':

I went to fetch her
From a friend's birthday party
In the long upper room of the Church Hall;
Some eleven-year-old lingerers were murdering
'Happy Birthday' on the old piano by the little platform;

There was a memento of iced cake in a twist of polythene
To take home, and there had been dancing;

There was still dancing,
The room was full of dancing, no girls were dancing,
There was dancing up to the ceiling, the air still paced
With Joy and I looked up and greeted them kindly.